Lincoln
Railway Stations

on old picture postcards

Eric Croft

1. Goxhill on the Humber bank. A pleasant view of the Great Central Railway buildings by local photographer West of Barrow-on-Humber. The card was posted to Portugal in November 1905.

**Designed and Published by
Reflections of a Bygone Age
Keyworth, Nottingham
1993**

£2.95

Lincolnshire railway stations featured in this book, with pre-grouping (1923) lines indicated.

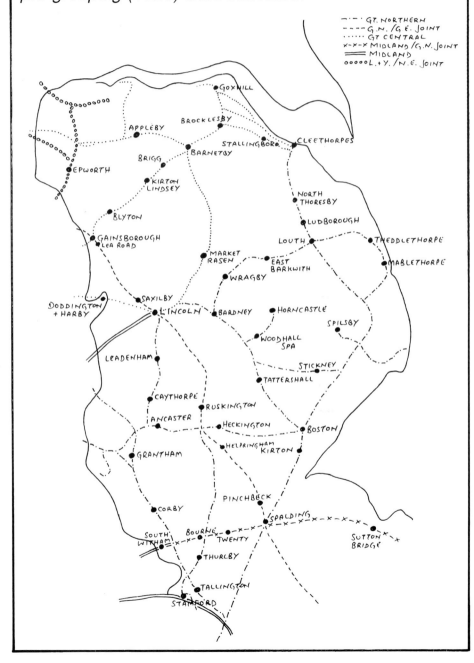

2. Brocklesby station on the Great Central about 1910. Three passengers are on the platform at the right and a goods train is approaching in the distance – otherwise activity is non-existent. An advert for 'Vim cleaner and polisher' is prominent. Brocklesby is still open for passenger traffic.

**Printed by
Adlard Print and Typesetting Services,
Ruddington, Notts.**

ISBN 0 946245 77 0

INTRODUCTION

The Great Northern Railway had established itself in Lincolnshire by the middle of the 19th century with lines linking most of the county's towns. The Great Central Railway was restricted to the north-east of the county and the Midland had a line to Lincoln from Nottinghamshire and another skirting the county in the south to Stamford and one or two villages.

The railways were responsible for the development of the Humber ports of Grimsby and Immingham, where the docks expanded rapidly, especially in the handling of coal exports: the volume of this trade increased some 40-fold between 1850 and 1910. With this development, the fishing industry was attracted to the ports, giving them even greater impetus. Boston, though, declined as a port with the coming of the railways. It had relied mainly on coasters carrying grain to London and the South but could not compete with the easy access, handling and speed of the railways. Similarly, the waterways in the county declined, though some of the canals were owned by the railway companies.

Goods traffic had been the rationale behind railway-building in Lincolnshire, but by the 1880s the carrying of passengers to the coastal resorts of Cleethorpes, Mablethorpe and Skegness became a major part of the railway's trade. The Great Northern carried almost a quarter of a million visitors to Skegness in the summer of 1882.

This book is not intended to be a history of railway stations in Lincolnshire, but a range of pictures giving a flavour of the Golden Age of Railways (and postcards). All the illustrations are from my collection of Lincolnshire cards: I'm sorry if I have not included your favourite local station – nor some of the important ones such as Grimsby, Scunthorpe and Sleaford – but regrettably not all the county's stations are in my postcard collection!

The boom years for picture postcards were from 1902-14, coinciding with excellent years for rail travel. Cards of stations, particularly the small local ones, are difficult to find, and because the postcard collector is competing with the railway enthusiast they have become expensive. Cards of the larger town and city stations were published by major national firms like W.H. Smith (whose cards always featured their own news-stands) but coverage of village stations was haphazard, depending on a keen local photographer. Publishers are mentioned in the captions where known.

Eric Croft
March 1993

Back cover (top): Bardney, on the Great Northern Line between Lincoln and Louth, also offered services to Woodhall Junction and Boston. It is seen here on a card by Gibson & Co. of Gateshead, published about 1906. Bardney closed to passengers in October 1970.

   (bottom): Leadenham.

3. Rather more activity at **Brocklesby** here! A collision on 27th March 1907 resulted in several tons of fish being deposited on the tracks and platform.

4. Appleby station on the Great Central. The postcard was sent to Louth in January 1924 though the writer evidently hadn't travelled by train, as the message reads *"Roads in horrible condition"*. The station is plastered with posters and adverts, including one for the *Sheffield Telegraph.* Appleby closed in 1967.

The Village Railway Station

The railway network was a mass of contradictions and contrasts, with the atmosphere at Lincoln, for example, as far removed from Leadenham or Spilsby as the M1 is from a country lane today. But all became part of the same inter-dependent network, and when branch lines were axed in the fifties and sixties, important feeder routes to the main system were lost. Lincolnshire, like everywhere else, had its remote stations, but has been fortunate in retaining at least two cross-country lines – to Skegness and Nottingham – where village stations have remained open. Their character, however, has gone for ever: now they are staffless halts – at Ancaster and Saxilby for example. Ninety years ago, though, when railways were the most frequently used transport, the village station was often the life and soul – economic, social and political – of the community it served. It was *"part of the district it served, with its own natural history, its own legends and folk lore, a staff who were at the heart of village affairs, its stations and adjoining pubs, places for exchange of gossip, news and advice."**

The country stationmaster would be among the most respected of village citizens, if not the most popular. He and his staff (often half-a-dozen or more) took great pride in the appearance of their station and the efficiency of their service, which would include receipt of mail, newspapers and all kinds of goods, as well as the safe carriage of people. Many country stations had the telegraph installed as early as 1868. Rural stops handled milk, animals for market, farm produce, beer, grain and a host of other articles. With its own buildings, including waiting-rooms, booking hall, staff rooms, toilets, sometimes even a refreshment room, with a signalbox, possibly and engine-shed, with a yard for goods deliveries, a well-kept garden, and staff houses, country stations were often almost self-contained communities!

* *The Country Railway – David St. John Thomas*

5. Stallingborough on the Great Central between Cleethorpes and Hull. In 1910, some 13 trains in each direction stopped there. On this card, posted at Lincoln in December 1906, a rather splendid carriage is outside the station, which is still in use today.

6. Cleethorpes station, at the end of the G.C. line. Not a very inspired photograph for a station boasting an ornate domed roof and elaborate clock tower. Postcard published by E.A. Schwerdtfeger of London, and posted from Nottingham in August 1913.

7. Barnetby, on the Lincoln-Cleethorpes Great Central Line. The card, published anonymously about 1910, is a classic railway station scene with engine no. 263 pulling in with a passenger train, and a goods passing through. Great Western excursions are advertised on the right.

GREAT CENTRAL RAILWAY STATION, BRIGG.

8. A W.H. Smith-published card of **Brigg,** on the Retford-Barnetby G.C. line, showing the station about 1906. On the left platform are weighing machine, trolley and news-stand, including a newspaper trailer *"Boy Scout killed at play"*.

9. Epworth was on the Axholme Joint Railway between Goole and Haxey Junction, and in Edwardian days received only three trains in each direction on weekdays (two extra on Saturdays). It closed to passenger trains in July 1933 and to goods in April 1965. Message on the reverse of the card (which was posted at Epworth in September 1904) reads: *"we really have a railway station at Epworth now. The latest report says the line is to be opened on 1st Nov. 1904, so we look forward to seeing you a little oftener when it is thoroughly working."* J. Bottomley of Epworth published the card.

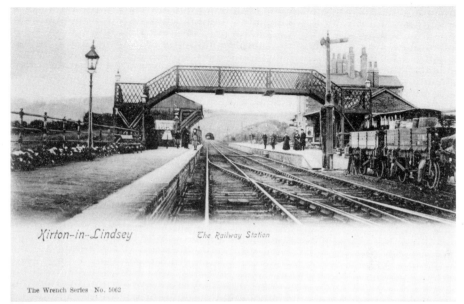

10. Kirton Lindsey on the Great Central is shown on a c.1904 card published by Wrench of London. The station is still in use.

11. R.N. Lister of Hull published this card of **Blyton** station on the Gainsborough-Barnetby Great Central line about 1910. With its slate roof and stone mullioned windows, it is typical of Victorian railway structures, which were built to last! The station, though, was closed to passengers in February 1959, and entirely in March 1964. An excursion to Cleethorpes is advertised on the poster.

12. North Thoresby on the Great Northern between Cleethorpes and Boston was closed in October 1970. Note the staggered platforms, level crossing and signal box. The station house on the left was built in 1847.

13. Ludborough was the next station up the line towards Louth, and has a similar arrangement to North Thoresby, with an almost identical station building. The postcard was published anonymously about 1910. Ludborough's last passenger train ran on 11th September 1961; goods traffic ceased in May 1964. Notice the ubiquitous 'Pears' advertisement.

Published by C. Parker, Louth.

14. Louth Great Northern station had an impressive facade. On this 1906 postcard, published locally by C. Parker, the Earl of Witham's coach from Elkington Hall dominates the scene. Louth closed in 1970.

15. Theddlethorpe, station for the village of Theddlethorpe-all-Saints, was on the single-track line from Louth to the coast, a Great Northern loop branch. Only five trains a day stopped there in 1910, however, and it is amazing that the station remained open for passenger traffic until December 1960. No indication of who published this card.

16. Mablethorpe survived for ten more years before it, too, fell victim to the axe of rationalisation. I wonder how many holiday trippers pounded the platforms during its 93-year life?

GREAT CENTRAL RAILWAY STATION, GAINSBOROUGH

17. W.H. Smith card of **Gainsborough Central,** posted to Lincoln in March 1910. *"We all went to the fair last night, but it was very quiet. I did not enjoy myself at all, but I am looking forward to Lincoln Fair,"* wrote Fred to Elsie Hoggett.

LEA ROAD STATION, GAINSBOROUGH.

18. Gainsborough's other station was **Lea Road**, on the Great Northern/Great Eastern joint line to Lincoln. It lost a goods facility in 1967, but still has a passenger service. Postcard published by the Halifax firm of Lilywhite.

19. Market Rasen, another Great Central Station, on an Edwardian card. A train has just pulled in and passengers are leaving the buildings. Note the water tower by the engine.

20. East Barkwith station on the Lincoln-Louth Great Northern line, with four railway staff and a beer barrel on the platform. This station closed to passengers in 1951, and completely in 1958.

21. Produced by the Cotswold Publishing Co. of Wotton-under-Edge, this view of **Wragby** station, next station up the line from East Barkwith, was published about 1912. It wasn't exactly a hive of activity then, and its passenger closure in 1951 could hardly have been unexpected.

S 5956 GREAT NORTHERN RAILWAY STATION, LINCOLN

22. Shunting by horse-power at **Lincoln Central** (the Great Northern/Great Central Joint Station) on another W.H. Smith postcard, sent from Lincoln to Woodford Green in November 1910. Of the two Lincoln stations, this one is still in use, but postcards of both are very difficult to find – rather surprising as they are only a few yards off the High Street.

23. Lincoln St. Marks about 1906 showing the massive portico entrance. This station has recently closed but the building is to be retained in the redevelopments. Trains left from here for Nottingham.

S 9089   G. N. RLY ST

24. Spilsby, a terminal station on a short Great No
1958. Postcard by W.H. Smith – note again the mass

SPILSBY.

 line, closed to passengers in 1939 and to all traffic in
verywhere.

A consignment of Albion & Deering Binders arrive at Horncastle Station
for E. Achurch & Sons.

25. Horncastle was at the end of a $7^1/2$ mile branch line off the Great Northern route
from Lincoln to Boston. This particular view, on a 1915 postcard, is possibly of more
interest to a farm machinery enthusiast, though! Horncastle station closed to passenger traffic in 1954.

Broadway, Woodhall Spa

26. Woodhall Spa is perhaps the commonest of all postcard views of Lincolnshire stations. This card of the station and Broadway was published about 1904.

27. Saxilby, on the Great Northern/Great Eastern Joint Railway between Lincoln and Gainsborough. It is still in use and little changed, apart from its lack of staff today! The postcard was sent to Lincoln in August 1905 with the message *"I shall come tomorrow evening by the train leaving here at 20 to 8..."*

28. Tattershall station on the Lincoln-Boston branch of the Great Northern. It sports a rather strange three-storey railway house on this c.1906 postcard. Tattershall was closed in June 1963 but the buildings have been refurbished and are now used as a craft centre.

29. Stickney, on what was known as the 15-mile Coningsby-Bellwater Junction line which connected the two Great Northern lines running north of Boston. The line was the last to be built in Lincolnshire, opening in 1913. Its five stations closed along with the line in October 1970.

Leadenham Station.

30. Leadenham was one of seven intermediate stations on the Great Northern Line from Grantham to Lincoln, and almost equidistant between the two. Seven passenger trains called in each direction on most days, with just a single one on Sundays, in 1910. The station was closed in 1965. Postcard published by R. Stevenett of nearby Caythorpe.

31. Ancaster was on the Grantham-Sleaford-Boston branch of the Great Northern, and is featured on a card posted from the village to Bolton in Lancashire in 1906. Note the ornate roof on the signalbox – more impressive than the station buildings! In Edwardian Days it hosted seven weekday passenger trains in each direction: there is a better service today, unusually.

32. There can't be too many stations with an eight-sailed windmill (or mill of any kind!) alongside, but **Heckington,** the other side of Sleaford on the same G.N. line, boasted a fine example. Both station and mill are currently in full operating order.

CAYTHORPE STATION

33. Caythorpe on the Great Northern Line from Lincoln to Grantham closed to passengers in September 1962 and goods trains two years later. Eight station staff are in evidence on this postcard, sent from Grantham in August 1908 – a generous allocation, with only five stopping passenger trains on most weekdays.

34. Ruskington about 1908 on an anonymously-published card, with staff and workmen posing for the photographer. A country station five miles west of Sleaford on the Great Northern/Great Eastern joint line to Lincoln, it was closed to passenger trains in 1961 but re-opened in 1975.

S 11640   G. N. RLY STATION BOSTON

35. Boston's Great Northern Station on a W.H. Smith postcard, sent to Rochdale from Alford in December 1915. The station is still in use, but with rather less impressive architecture and facilities than featured on this postcard, where the W.H. Smith bookstall dominated the far platform.

36. Kirton near Boston, pictured about 1905 in a track-level view. The station platforms are staggered, with a level crossing in between, and another ornate signalbox. This Great Northern station was closed in the early 1960s.

S 9100   G. N. R. STATION, GRANTHAM.

37. W.H. Smith promoted cards of stations where their own bookstall was featured, and **Grantham** (G.N.R.) was no exception. On the East Coast main line, it was – and still is – the busiest of Lincolnshire's railway stations.

38. Claypole was on the Great Northern's east coast main line, five miles south of Newark. It was only granted six stopping trains in each direction on weekdays (one on Sunday) in Edwardian times, but saw plenty of activity on a very busy route. It lost its passenger service in September 1957 and closed entirely in July 1964.

39. Pinchbeck, two miles out of Spalding towards Sleaford on the G.N./G.E. joint line. Six passenger trains called each way on weekdays in Edwardian times, but the station buildings were quite elaborate for such a rural place. It closed to passengers in September 1961 and goods in December 1964. The card, of c.1910 vintage, was published by Beales and Son of Spalding.

40. South Witham on the Saxby-Bourne branch of the Midland and Great Northern Joint Railway (four passenger trains a day each way in 1910) had a thriving goods yard, as seen on this card. The line single-tracked either side of the station.

41. Twenty station, between Bourne and Spalding, showing another flood on a card by Williamson. The station, which existed in isolation – there was no village there – closed in 1959.

Spalding Railway Station.

42. Spalding Great Northern station on a card by the "Free Press", sent to Felixstowe in October 1910. The photograph shows a busy scene, with no fewer than five trains at the platforms.

43. Passengers could travel from **Bourne** in four directions in Edwardian days, either on the Great Northern line or on the G.N./Midland joint. As the well-stocked bookstall and crowded platform shows (though the station staff outnumber passengers!) it was a busy place. Passenger services, though, fell victim to the axe in 1959. No indication of who published this postcard.

44. Helpringham, on the G.N./G.E. joint between Sleaford and Spalding, hosted five weekday trains each way in 1907 when this postcard was published. Passenger traffic ceased in July 1955, goods in December 1964.

45. A fine panoramic view of **Sutton Bridge,** between Spalding and Kings Lynn. Trains also ran south to Wisbech. The Midland/Great Northern joint station was an impressive affair, as befitted its junction status.

46. A photo from line level showing the island platform and station building, and the large station sign.

47. Thurlby, between Bourne and Essendine on the Great Northern, shown on a c.1910 postcard. This was quite a busy line, with eight passenger trains each way daily at the time. It closed to both passenger and goods traffic in June 1951. One of the posters advertises Woodhall Spa, featuring a picture of healthy pine woods and bracing moorland.

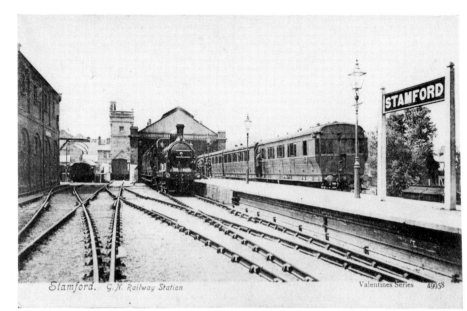

Stamford. G.N. Railway Station   Valentines Series 49958

48. Valentine-published card of **Stamford** (Great Northern) station, posted to Hull in March 1906. Lincolnshire's most southerly station and one of two in the town, it closed to passengers in March 1957 and goods traffic six years later.

TALLINGTON STATION. 236A

49. An empty **Tallington** station about 1907 – but just look at the mass of posters on the walls! On the Great Northern's east coast main line between Peterborough and Essendine, it was closed in 1959.